FIGURE 2. Study areas based on Hammond Land Surface Forms and state boundaries. Coastal Zone and Great Lakes strata were added to facilitate sampling design. (Hammond, 1965)

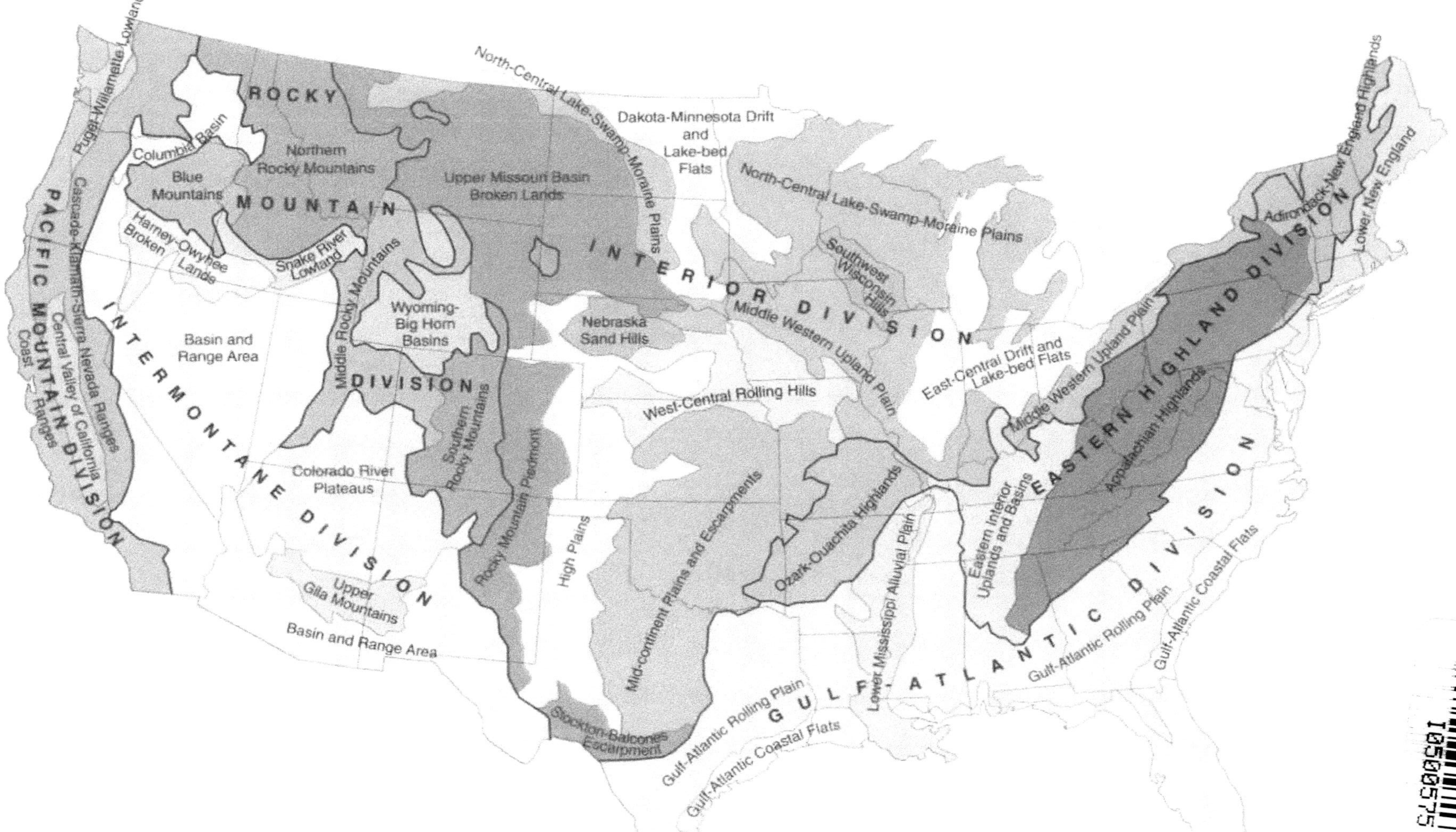

Wetlands

STATUS AND TRENDS IN THE CONTERMINOUS UNITED STATES MID-1970's TO MID-1980's

First Update of the National
Wetlands Status Report

1991

By
Thomas E. Dahl
U.S. Fish and Wildlife Service
National Wetlands Inventory
St. Petersburg, Florida

and

Craig E. Johnson
U.S. Fish and Wildlife Service
Division of Habitat Conservation

Statistical Data Analysis by
W.E. Frayer
Michigan Technological University
Houghton, Michigan

This report should be cited as follows:

Dahl, T.E. and C.E. Johnson. 1991. *Status and Trends of Wetlands in the Conterminous United States, Mid-1970's to Mid-1980's.* U.S. Department of the Interior, Fish and Wildlife Service, Washington, D.C. 28 pages.

PREFACE

The U.S. Fish and Wildlife Service is the principal Federal agency with responsibility for protecting and managing the Nation's fish and wildlife and their habitats. Because of the importance of wetlands to the Nation's fish and wildlife, the Service is particularly concerned with the fate of wetlands and associated deepwater habitats. In 1982, the Fish and Wildlife Service's National Wetlands Inventory completed a study of the status and trends of wetlands and deepwater habitats for the conterminous United States. The 1982 report estimated the acreage of wetlands remaining in the conterminous United States and the changes in wetland acreage between the mid-1950's and the mid-1970's.

The Emergency Wetlands Resources Act of 1986 requires the Fish and Wildlife Service to update the initial wetlands status and trends information every ten years, beginning with this report. This report is the first national update of the 1982 report and was prepared to fulfill the statutory requirements of the Act.

This report does not address the causes for changes in wetland acreage or the effects those changes may have had on the Nation's fish and wildlife resources. A subsequent report is being prepared that will provide a more comprehensive analysis of the data presented in this report.

Wetlands, as measured by the status and trends study, are defined by the Fish and Wildlife Service's wetlands classification system Cowardin, et. al. 1979, that defines the biological extent of wetlands using various techniques including high altitude aerial photography. It includes both vegetated and non-vegetated wetlands. References to this wetlands definition and terminology are found in Appendix A of this report.

This report uses one methodology (based on the Cowardin, et. al. classification system) for identifying and classifying wetlands. We recognize that other government reports may use different methodologies.

The Federal Manual for Identifying and Delineating Jurisdictional Wetlands delineates wetlands based on precise on-the-ground measurement techniques and focuses only on vegetated wetlands.

This report is the result of extensive effort by many individuals throughout the U.S. Fish and Wildlife Service. Special appreciation is extended to Dr. Donald Woodard, Group Leader, Dr. H. Ross Pywell, Mr.

*   *Present affiliation: South Florida Water Management District, West Palm Beach, Florida*

Herman Robinson, Ms. Renee Whitehead, Mr. Norman Mangrum, Ms. Rebecca Stanley, Ms. Georgann Shylkofski, Ms. Gwendolyn Sanderlin, and Mr. Leslie Vilchek* of the National Wetlands Inventory Group, St. Petersburg, Florida; Mr. Charles Storrs of the Division of Habitat Conservation in Atlanta, Georgia; Dr. Bill O. Wilen, Project Leader, Mr. Carlos Mendoza, and Ms. Mary Bates, National Wetlands Inventory, Washington, D.C.; Ms. Denise Henne, Office of Correspondence and Information, Washington, D.C.; Dr. W.E. Frayer, School of Forestry, Michigan Technological University, Houghton, Michigan; Mr. Keith Patterson and Mr. Jim Dick, of Geonex-Martel, Inc. Special recognition is also due to Mr. William Knapp and Ms. Cathy Short, Division of Habitat Conservation, Washington, D.C., and Ms. E. LaVerne Smith, Branch of Special Projects, Washington, D.C.

TABLE OF CONTENTS

LIST OF TABLES

LIST OF FIGURES

EXECUTIVE SUMMARY

The Emergency Wetlands Resources Act of 1986 [16 U.S.C. 3931(a)] requires the Secretary of the Interior, acting through the Director of the Fish and Wildlife Service, to produce updated reports on the status and trends of wetlands and deepwater habitats in the conterminous United States, on a ten year cycle. This report is the first update of an earlier report titled Status and Trends of Wetlands and Deepwater Habitats in the Conterminous United States, 1950's to 1970's, which was completed in 1982. It constitutes a statistically valid effort to estimate the Nation's wetland resources and provide indications of gains or losses for 14 categories of wetland and deepwater habitats.

The sampling design consisted of a stratified random sample of 3,629 plots located within the lower 48 States. Aerial photography from the mid-1970's and the mid-1980's (mean dates were 1974 and 1983) was acquired for each of the plots and analyzed to detect changes in wetland acreage. Changes in the acreage of wetland and deepwater habitats were recorded as either natural or man-induced. The overall study design was intended to produce estimates of our Nation's wetlands at two points in time—the mid-1970's and mid-1980's.

The design recognized that aerial photography is not available in each successive year for the same plot or necessarily in the same year for all plots. For these reasons, estimates of average annual rates of wetland loss have not been developed by this study.

One possible way of calculating an average annual net loss of wetlands for the study period would be to use the wetland acreage estimate for the mid-1980's (1983) minus the acreage estimate for the mid-1970's (1974) and divide by the nine-year study period. Using this method, the average annual loss of wetlands for this period would be approximately 290 thousand acres.

The make-up of wetlands by vegetated cover type differs dramatically from freshwater to estuarine systems. In coastal areas, 73.1 percent of all wetlands were estuarine emergent whereas inland, an estimated 52.9 percent of freshwater wetlands were forested. Freshwater emergent marshes and shrubs make up 25.1 and 15.7 percent of the total freshwater wetlands, respectively.

Study results indicate that there were an estimated 105.9 million acres of wetlands in the conterminous United States in the mid-1970's. In the mid-1980's, there were 103.3 million acres of wetlands. This translates into a net loss of over 2.6 million acres over the study period. Freshwater wetlands experienced 98.0 percent of the losses that occurred during the study period. By the mid-1980's, an estimated 97.8 million acres of freshwater wetlands and 5.5 million acres of estuarine (coastal) wetlands remained.

Losses in the estuarine system were evident by the decrease in estuarine vegetated wetlands, which declined by 71.0 thousand acres. The majority of these losses occurred in the Gulf Coast States, and most of the loss was due to shifting of emergent wetlands to open salt water (bays). An estimated 57.0 percent of the losses of emergent salt marsh vegetation went to open salt water. Estuarine nonvegetated wetlands increased by an estimated 11.6 thousand acres from the mid-1970's to the mid-1980's.

Inland, palustrine (freshwater) vegetated wetlands experienced substantial losses. An estimated 3.3 million acres were lost from all palustrine (freshwater) vegetated categories from the mid-1970's to the mid-1980's. The area of palustrine nonvegetated wetlands (primarily freshwater ponds) increased by an estimated 792.4 thousand acres from the mid-1970's to the mid-1980's. Almost all of this increase was in palustrine unconsolidated bottom (primarily ponds), and most occurred on lands not previously classified as wetlands or deepwater habitats.

Wetland losses from the mid-1970's to the mid-1980's were more evenly distributed between agricultural land use and "other" land use (than from the 1950's to the mid-1970's). Conversions to agricultural land uses accounted for 54.0 percent of the losses while conversions to "other" land uses accounted for 41.0 percent of the losses. This is an appreciable change from trends observed in the earlier study in which agricultural conversion represented 87.0 percent of all wetland losses. A substantial portion of the increased importance of lands classified as "other" is attributable to wetlands that had been cleared and drained, but not yet put to an identifiable use. Conversions of wetlands to urban land uses accounted for about 5.0 percent of the wetlands loss. Overall, wetland acreage in the mid-1980's constituted 5.0 percent of the land area of the conterminous United States.

Since the mid-1980's, indications are that wetland losses are slowing. From 1987 to 1990, programs to restore wetlands under the 1985 Food Security Act have added about 90.0 thousand acres to the Nation's wetlands inventory (U.S. Fish and Wildlife Service 1991). Other programs to protect wetlands, like the Swampbuster provision of the Food Security Act, have generated support for conserving wetlands. In addition, public education and extension efforts have helped heighten our Nation's awareness of the values of wetlands.

FIGURE 1. States that lost more than 50 percent of their wetlands between the 1780's and mid-1980's (Listed states shaded) (after Dahl 1990):

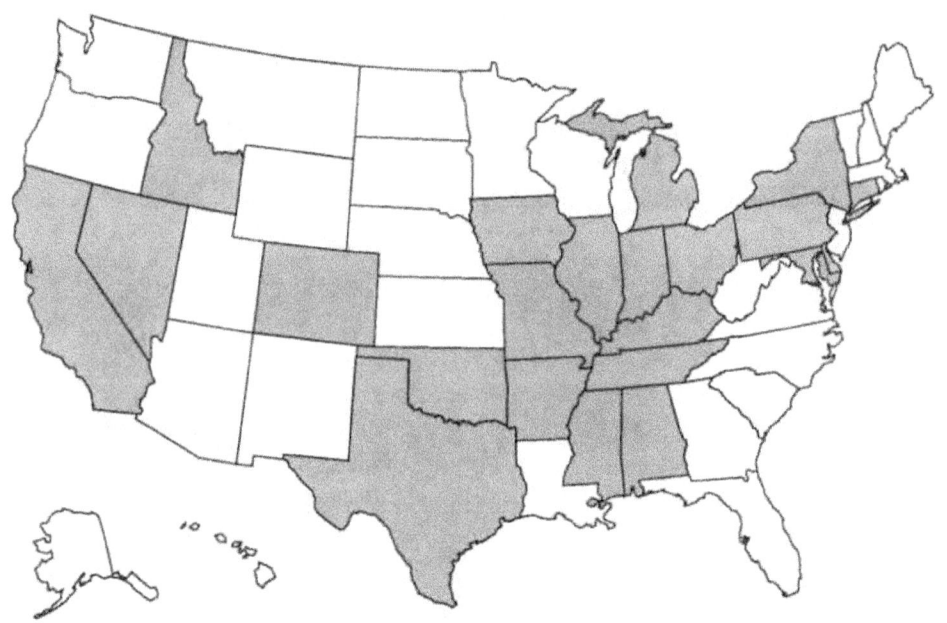

State	Percent Lost	State	Percent Lost
Alabama	50	Maryland	73
Arkansas	72	Michigan	50
California	91	Mississippi	59
Colorado	50	Missouri	87
Connecticut	74	Nevada	52
Delaware	54	New York	60
Idaho	56	Ohio	90
Illinois	85	Oklahoma	67
Indiana	87	Pennsylvania	56
Iowa	89	Tennessee	59
Kentucky	81	Texas	52

INTRODUCTION

Wetlands are critical ecosystems in the landscapes of America. They help regulate and maintain the hydrology of our Nation's rivers, lakes, and streams by storing and slowly releasing flood waters. They help maintain the quality of our Nation's water by storing nutrients, reducing sediment loads, and reducing erosion (Kusler and Brooks 1987, Mitsch and Gosselink 1986).

Wetlands are also critical to the fish and wildlife populations of America. They provide important habitat for about one third of the plant and animal species Federally listed as threatened or endangered. They also provide essential nesting, migratory, and wintering areas for more than 50 percent of the Nation's migratory bird species (U.S. Fish and Wildlife Service 1990a). Every year, countless shorebirds, egrets, herons, terns, gulls, pelicans, and other birds use the marshes, swamps, mud flats and other tidal areas, sloughs, and potholes that compose the Nation's wetlands. Millions of other fish and wildlife also depend on wetlands from northern Alaska to southern Florida.

At the time of Colonial America, the area that is now the conterminous United States contained an estimated 221 million acres of wetlands* (Dahl, 1990). Over a 200-year period, wetlands have been drained, dredged, filled, leveled and flooded. Twenty-two States have lost 50 percent or more of their original wetlands since the 1780's (Figure 1). Ten States—Arkansas, California, Connecticut, Illinois, Indiana, Iowa, Kentucky, Maryland, Missouri and Ohio—have lost 70 percent or more of their original wetland acreage.

In recent years, the Nation's appreciation of the ecological, social, and economic values of wetlands has increased dramatically (The Conservation Foundation 1988). This increased appreciation, combined with an awareness of how much wetland acreage had been converted or damaged since Colonial times, resulted in the development of wetlands protection legislation and programs. The Clean Water Act, and Presidential Executive Order 11990 are the most notable examples.

The Service's first wetlands status and trends report (Frayer et al. 1983a) estimated the rate of wetland conversion between the mid-1950's and the mid-1970's. For the most part, those estimates captured trends from the period preceding intensive efforts to protect and restore wetlands in the United States. In the interim period of time, there has been speculation about the effectiveness of government programs and policies that regulate or discourage wetland use (Barnard et al. 1985).

This report covers the mid-1970's to the mid-1980's, a period in which Federal, State, and local government programs and policies began to affect wetland use and conversion. For this reason, there has been intense interest by the scientific and governmental communities in these updated wetlands statistics (Dahl and Pywell 1989). Although the data contained in this report generally predates more recent wetlands legislation (e.g., Food Security Act, North American Wetlands Conservation Act), they provide information that can help to assess the effectiveness of public policies and programs that have been intended to reduce the loss of the Nation's remaining wetlands.

---

* A glossary of the terms used to classify wetlands in this study is presented in Appendix A.

SURVEY PROCEDURES

The Service's wetlands status and trends reports have one primary objective: produce comprehensive, statistically valid estimates of the Nation's wetlands acreage. To achieve this objective, a group of statisticians from the Fish and Wildlife Service, Forest Service, Soil Conservation Service, and the Army Corps of Engineers developed a design for a national wetlands status and trends study. This design was used for both the 1982 wetlands status and trends study and this update of that study. Several authors have also adapted the national study design to produce regional wetlands status reports (Frayer et al. 1989, Hall 1988, Tiner 1987).

STUDY DESIGN

The design for the national wetlands status and trends study consists of a stratified random sample of 3,629 plots. Each sample plot is four square miles, or 2,560 acres in size, and is permanent (i.e., the 1982 and 1991 status and trends studies use the same sample plots).

The conterminous United States was stratified using state boundaries and the 35 physical subdivisions described by Hammond (1970). Two additional strata were added to enhance the study design—a coastal stratum that consists of estuarine wetlands in coastal areas and a stratum encompassing the coastal areas of the Great Lakes (Figure 2, Inside Front Cover). Sample plots were randomly allocated to strata in proportion to the amount of wetland acreage expected in the stratum based on estimates developed by Shaw and Fredine (1956). As a result, the study design more intensively sampled areas where wetland habitats were more variable and had higher density (Figure 3).

This study was designed to be a quantitative measure of the areal extent of wetlands in the conterminous United States. It provides no indication of wetland quality outside of the diminishing area of wetlands, by category.

STATISTICAL RELIABILITY

National estimates were developed using the statistical procedures presented by Frayer et al. (1983a, 1983b). This study was designed to generate national acreage estimates and be 90 percent certain that those estimates were within 10 percent of the actual wetland acreage totals for the entire conterminous United States. The reliability of each estimate is expressed as a percent standard error for that estimate. Where statistical reliability permitted, regional or state estimates were developed.

PROCEDURES

To collect information for each of the sample plots, the Service acquired U.S. Geological Survey topographic maps and aerial photography for the study period. The mean years of the aerial photography used in this study were 1974 and 1983 (Table 1); this nine-year interval may be used as the basis for calculating annual average acreage estimates. Typically, the imagery used for the 1980's was color infrared photography, while the imagery used for the 1970's was black and white photography.

All aerial photographs were interpreted and annotated using the procedures developed by the National Wetlands Inventory (U.S. Fish and Wildlife Service 1990b; 1990c). The photo interpretation assigned wetlands and deepwater habitats observed on the aerial photographs to one of the 14 categories listed in Table 2. All changes were recorded as either natural (e.g., natural conversions of emergent wetlands to shrub wetlands) or man-induced (e.g., conversion of wetlands to a

TABLE 1. Mean dates of the photographic coverage for the sample plots used in this study, by State.

State	1970's	1980's	State	1970's	1980's
Alabama	1975	1981	Nebraska	1975	1983
Arizona	1973	1982	Nevada	1974	1981
Arkansas	1974	1983	New Hampshire	1974	1986
California	1974	1983	New Jersey	1978	1984
Colorado	1976	1982	New Mexico	1975	1982
Connecticut	1972	1985	New York	1974	1985
Delaware	1977	1982	North Carolina	1973	1983
Florida	1974	1984	North Dakota	1975	1983
Georgia	1975	1982	Ohio	1972	1982
Idaho	1976	1982	Oklahoma	1975	1983
Illinois	1973	1982	Oregon	1975	1982
Indiana	1973	1983	Pennsylvania	1971	1983
Iowa	1975	1983	Rhode Island	1976	1985
Kansas	1972	1982	South Carolina	1973	1983
Kentucky	1974	1982	South Dakota	1974	1983
Louisiana	1974	1983	Tennessee	1972	1981
Maine	1975	1984	Texas	1974	1983
Maryland	1972	1982	Utah	1975	1984
Massachusetts	1971	1985	Vermont	1975	1986
Michigan	1974	1982	Virginia	1974	1982
Minnesota	1975	1983	Washington	1975	1982
Mississippi	1973	1982	West Virginia	1975	1984
Missouri	1973	1983	Wisconsin	1974	1981
Montana	1974	1982	Wyoming	1977	1981

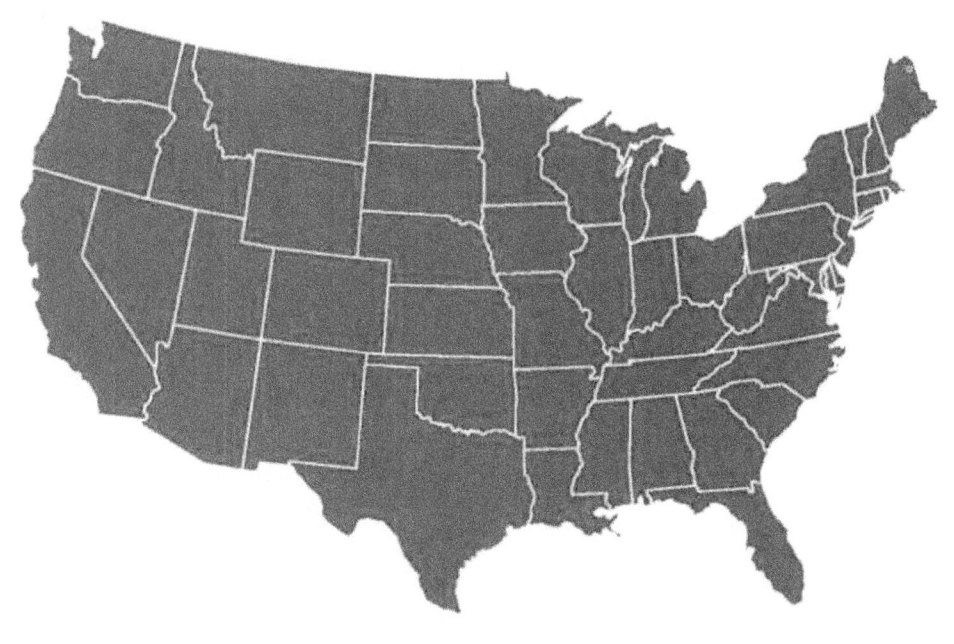

nonwetland area like agriculture or urban development). Areas in sample plots that were previously identified as wetlands but were no longer wetlands were placed into three broad land use categories: agricultural, urban, and "other."

Once the interpretation was complete, zoom transfer scopes were used to transfer the data from the aerial photographs to overlays on U.S. Geological Survey 1:24,000 scale topographic maps. Changes in wetland area between the mid-1970's and the mid-1980's were determined on these maps. All photo interpretation and data compilation for this study were completed by August, 1990.

Quality control checks were built into the process to prevent false changes from being recorded and to provide confirmation of the photo interpretation work. Acreage determinations and data entry provided further quality assurance to the raw plot data.

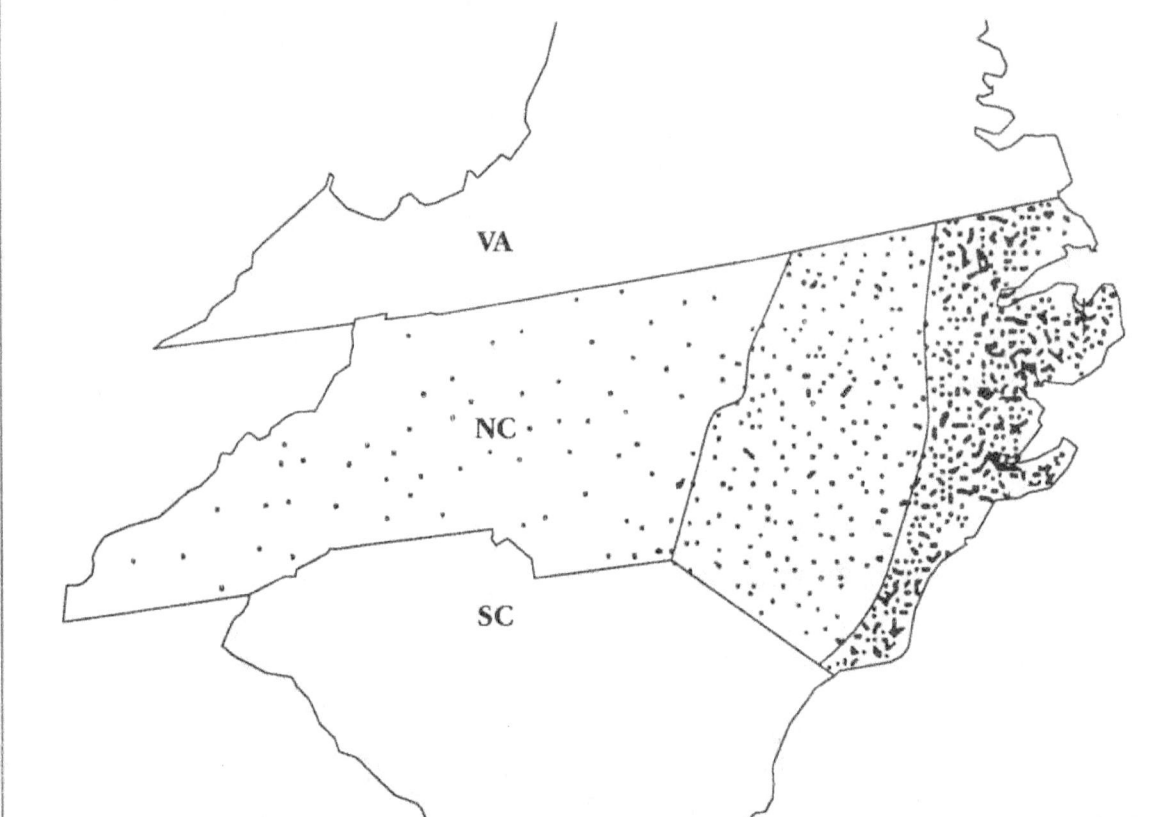

FIGURE 3.
Sample plot distribution for the State of North Carolina. Coastal areas with more habitat variability and suspected wetland density are more intensively sampled than mountainous areas.

TABLE 2. Wetland, deepwater, and upland habitat categories used in this study.

Salt Water Habitats*   **Common Description**

Marine Intertidal   Nearshore

Estuarine Subtidal**   Open water/baybottoms

Estuarine Intertidal Emergents   Salt marsh

Estuarine Intertidal Forested/Shrub   Mangroves or other estuarine shrubs

Estuarine Intertidal Unconsolidated Shore   Beaches/bars

Estuarine Subtidal Unconsolidated Bottom   Open water estuary

Riverine** (may be tidal or non-tidal)   River systems

Freshwater Habitats*

Palustrine Forested   Forested swamps/bogs

Palustrine Shrub   Shrub wetlands

Palustrine Emergents   Inland marshes/wet meadows

Palustrine Unconsolidated Shore   Shore beaches/bars

Palustrine Unconsolidated Bottom   Open water ponds

Palustrine Aquatic Bed   Floating aquatic or submerged vegetation

Lacustrine**   Lakes/reservoirs

Upland Land Use

Agriculture   Crop agriculture/pasture

Urban   Built-up/developments

Other Uplands   Rural uplands not in agriculture
                                                  or pasturelands.

---

*   *Adapted from Cowardin et al. (1979) See Appendix A*

** *Includes deepwater habitats*

RESULTS

This study produced estimates of wetland acreage changes from the mid-1970's to the mid-1980's for 14 wetland and deepwater categories. These data are presented in Appendix B and are summarized in Table 3.

NATIONAL STATUS

In the mid-1970's, there were an estimated 105.9 million acres of wetlands in the conterminous United States. In the mid-1980's, an estimated 103.3 million acres of wetlands remained.

Of the remaining wetland acreage in the conterminous United States, 97.8 million acres or 95.0 percent were freshwater (inland) wetlands. Another 5.5 million acres (5.0 percent) were estuarine (coastal) wetlands. In coastal areas, 73.1 percent of all estuarine wetlands were emergent marshes. Another 12.7 percent were estuarine forested/shrubs. Sandy or rock shorelines represented 9.9 percent of the coastal wetland acreage, while estuarine aquatic beds represented 4.3 percent (Figure 4).

Inland, 52.9 percent of all palustrine wetlands were forested. Freshwater emergent marshes made up 25.1 percent; 15.7 percent were wetlands dominated by shrubs. Freshwater ponds represented an estimated 5.7 percent of the total, with less than 0.6 percent of the acreage represented by other freshwater wetland categories (Figure 5).

The acreage of deepwater habitats was also included in this study. There were an estimated 63.0 million acres of deepwater habitat in the lacustrine and riverine systems in the mid-1980's. This represents an increase of 271.2 thousand acres from the mid-1970's estimate and was primarily due to the construction of reservoirs and lakes in the southeastern States of Alabama, Florida, Georgia, Mississippi, and South Carolina.

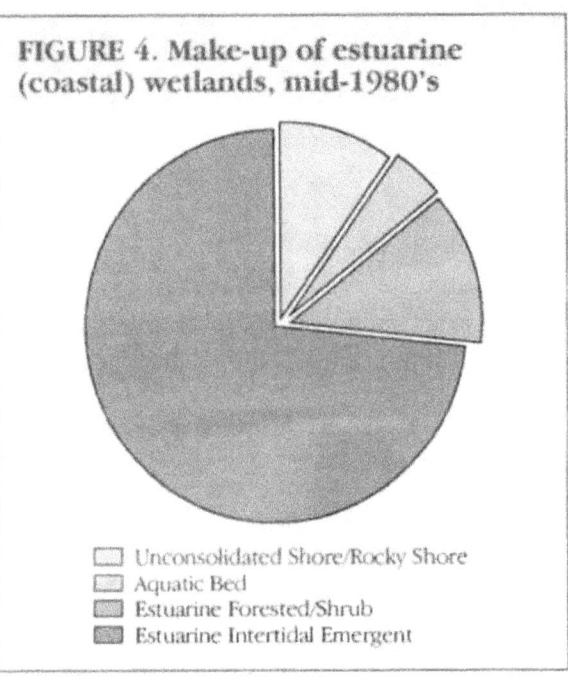

FIGURE 4. Make-up of estuarine (coastal) wetlands, mid-1980's

☐ Unconsolidated Shore/Rocky Shore
☐ Aquatic Bed
▨ Estuarine Forested/Shrub
▨ Estuarine Intertidal Emergent

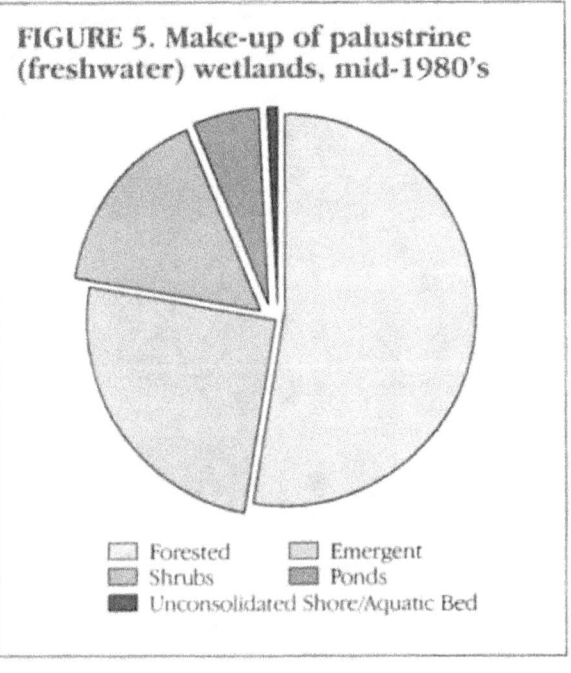

FIGURE 5. Make-up of palustrine (freshwater) wetlands, mid-1980's

☐ Forested ☐ Emergent
▨ Shrubs ▨ Ponds
■ Unconsolidated Shore/Aquatic Bed

TABLE 3. Gains and losses for selected categories of wetlands and deepwater habitats, mid-1970's to mid-1980's. The standard error for each entry, expressed as a percentage of the entry, is given in parenthesis. A standard error greater or equal to an estimate is represented by an asterisk.

Wetland Category	Acres in 1,000's			
	Estimated Acreage Mid-1970's	*Estimated Acreage Mid-1980's*	*Acreage Change Mid-1970's to Mid-1980's*	*Percent Change*
Estuarine Intertidal Non-vegetated[1]	678.2 (11.8)	689.8 (11.6)	11.6 (36.3)	1.7
Estuarine Intertidal Vegetated[2]	4,853.9 (4.2)	4,782.9 (4.2)	−71.0 (18.2)	−1.5
All Estuarine Wetlands[3]	5,532.1 (3.9)	5,472.7 (4.0)	−59.4 (22.7)	−1.1
Palustrine Non-vegetated[4]	5,348.9 (20.9)	6,141.3 (18.5)	792.4 (25.5)	14.8
Palustrine Emergent	24,312.8 (8.6)	24,533.0 (8.6)	220.2 *	—
Palustrine Forested	55,151.2 (3.2)	51,747.8 (3.4)	−3,403.4 (8.9)	−6.2
Palustrine Shrub	15,505.6 (6.4)	15,344.5 (6.4)	−161.1 *	—
Palustrine Vegetated Wetlands[5]	94,969.6 (3.3)	91,625.3 (3.4)	−3,344.3 (14.6)	−3.5
All Palustrine Wetlands[6]	100,318.5 (3.3)	97,766.6 (3.5)	−2,551.9 (20.7)	−2.5
All Estuarine and Palustrine Wetlands	105,850.6 (3.1)	103,239.3 (3.3)	−2,611.3 (20.3)	−2.5
Lacustrine	57,639.7 (11.4)	57,842.8 (11.3)	203.1 (48.7)	0.4
Riverine	5,123.0 (10.9)	5,191.1 (11.0)	68.1 *	—
Estuarine Subtidal	18,852.4 (2.5)	18,882.4 (2.5)	30.0 (31.5)	0.2
All Deepwater Habitats[7]	81,615.1 (8.0)	81,916.3 (8.0)	301.2 (40.9)	0.4
All Wetlands and Deepwater Habitats[8]	187,570.2 (3.9)	185,259.9 (4.0)	−2,310.3 (23.4)	−1.2

[1] *Includes the categories: Estuarine intertidal unconsolidated shore, and Estuarine intertidal aquatic beds.*
[2] *Includes the categories: Estuarine intertidal emergent and Estuarine intertidal forested and scrub/shrub wetlands*
[3] *All Estuarine intertidal categories*
[4] *Includes the categories: Palustrine unconsolidated bottom, Palustrine unconsolidated shores, Palustrine aquatic beds*
[5] *Includes the categories: Palustrine emergent, Palustrine forested, and Palustrine scrub/shrub wetlands*
[6] *Includes all Palustrine categories*
[7] *Includes all Estuarine subtidal, Lacustrine, and Riverine deepwater*
[8] *Includes Marine intertidal wetlands*

Wetlands represent approximately 5.0 percent of the land area in the lower 48 States. If wetlands and deepwater acres were combined, about 9.3 percent of the land area in the conterminous United States is made up of these areas.

TRENDS IN WETLAND RESOURCES, MID-1970'S TO MID-1980'S

Estuarine wetlands

The acreage of estuarine wetlands declined 1.0 percent between the mid-1970's and the mid-1980's (Table 4). By far the most dramatic impact to coastal wetlands was the loss of 70.9 thousand acres of estuarine emergent wetlands, primarily in the Gulf Coast States. However, this figure does not encompass all of the coastal wetland losses

during the study period because some coastal areas contain extensive palustrine emergent and palustrine forested wetlands. Many of these palustrine wetlands were converted to non-palustrine wetlands, open water, upland, or deepwater habitats during the study period. Therefore, the loss of coastal wetlands in states like Louisiana cannot be derived solely from losses of estuarine intertidal emergent wetlands.

The fate of these conversions is shown in Figure 6. A net loss of 40.4 thousand acres (57.0 percent) of estuarine emergent marshes resulted from conversions to open salt water. The overall net loss of estuarine wetlands for the study period was estimated at 59.4 thousand acres.

Acres of estuarine shrub wetlands appeared to be stable, with no statistically significant change detected between the mid-1970's and mid-1980's. Estuarine unconsolidated shores increased in area

TABLE 4. Changes in coastal wetland acreage, mid-1970's to mid-1980's (Acres are in 1,000's). The standard error for each entry, expressed as a percentage of the entry, is given in parenthesis. A standard error greater or equal to an estimate is represented by an asterisk.

Wetland Category	Estimated Acreage Mid-1970's	Estimated Acreage Mid-1980's	Acreage Change Mid-1970's to Mid-1980's	Mid-1980's Acreage As Percent of All Coastal Acreage
Marine Intertidal	104.5 (22.0)	104.3 (22.0)	−0.2	1.9
Estuarine Emergent	4,144.9 (4.2)	4,074.0 (4.2)	−70.9 (18.2)	73.1
Estuarine Forested/Shrub	709.0 (13.5)	709.0 (13.4)	0.0	12.7
Estuarine Shore	430.3 (12.3)	448.1 (11.9)	17.8 (42.7)	8.0
Estuarine Aquatic bed	247.9 (21.8)	241.7 (22.1)	−6.2 *	4.3
Estuarine Intertidal Nonvegetated[1]	678.2 (11.8)	689.8 (11.6)	11.6 (36.2)	12.6
Estuarine Intertidal Vegetated[2]	4,853.9 (4.2)	4,782.9 (4.2)	−71.0 (18.2)	87.4
Changes in coastal deepwater acreage mid-1970's to mid-1980's				
Estuarine Subtidal	18,852.4 (2.5)	18,882.4 (2.5)	30.0 (31.5)	—

[1] *Includes the categories: Estuarine intertidal unconsolidated shore and Estuarine intertidal aquatic bed*
[2] *Includes the categories: Estuarine intertidal emergent and Estuarine forested and scrub/shrub*

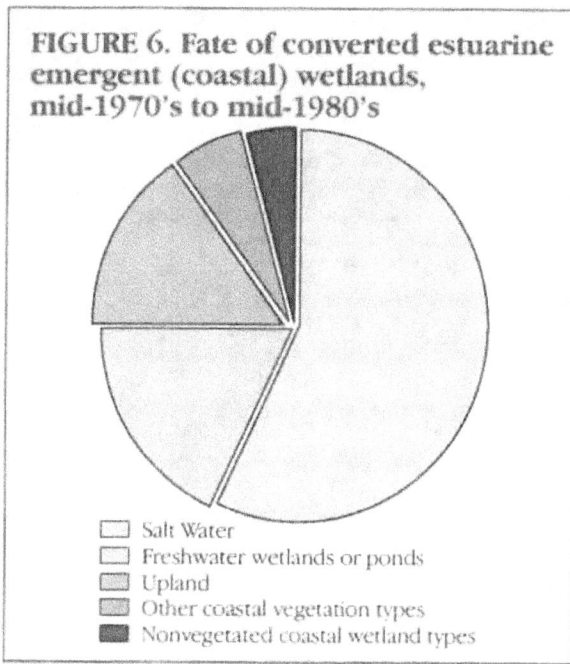

FIGURE 6. Fate of converted estuarine emergent (coastal) wetlands, mid-1970's to mid-1980's

☐ Salt Water
☐ Freshwater wetlands or ponds
☐ Upland
☐ Other coastal vegetation types
■ Nonvegetated coastal wetland types

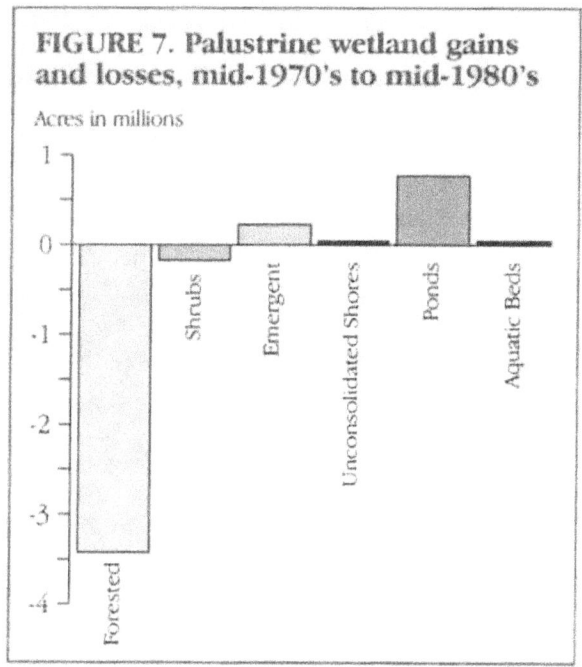

FIGURE 7. Palustrine wetland gains and losses, mid-1970's to mid-1980's

by 17.8 thousand acres from the mid-1970's estimate.

The acreage of estuarine subtidal deepwater increased by 53.2 thousand acres as a result of conversions of what had been estuarine emergent marsh in the mid-1970's. Conversely, only 12.8 thousand acres of what had been estuarine subtidal deepwater became estuarine emergents in the mid-1980's and 10.4 thousand acres ultimately became other wetland categories. Overall, there was a 30.0 thousand acre increase in estuarine subtidal deepwater.

Changes in marine intertidal wetlands were not statistically significant.

Palustrine wetlands

From the mid-1970's to mid-1980's, palustrine wetlands decreased by nearly 2.5 million acres. Palustrine forested wetlands suffered the biggest loss during the study period. An estimated 3.4 million acres were converted (Figure 7), primarily in the southern portion of the country (Figures 8 and 9). Over 2.1 million acres of these wetlands were converted to non-wetland land uses, including about 1.0 million acres that were lost to agriculture. Most of the remaining acreage was converted from palustrine forested wetlands to other wetland categories.

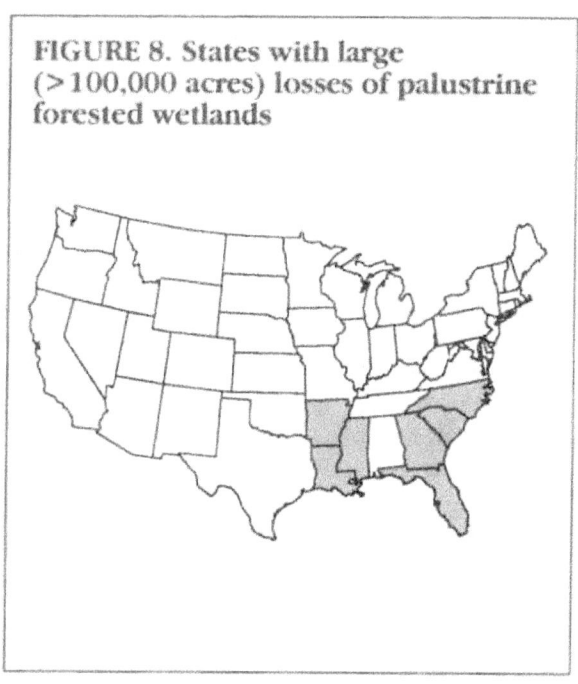

FIGURE 8. States with large (>100,000 acres) losses of palustrine forested wetlands

Overall, palustrine emergent wetlands increased by 220.2 thousand acres during the study period (Figure 7). About 375.2 thousand acres of palustrine emergent wetlands were converted to agricultural land uses, 151.2 thousand acres were converted to "other" land uses, and 37.5 thousand acres were converted to urban land uses. An addi-

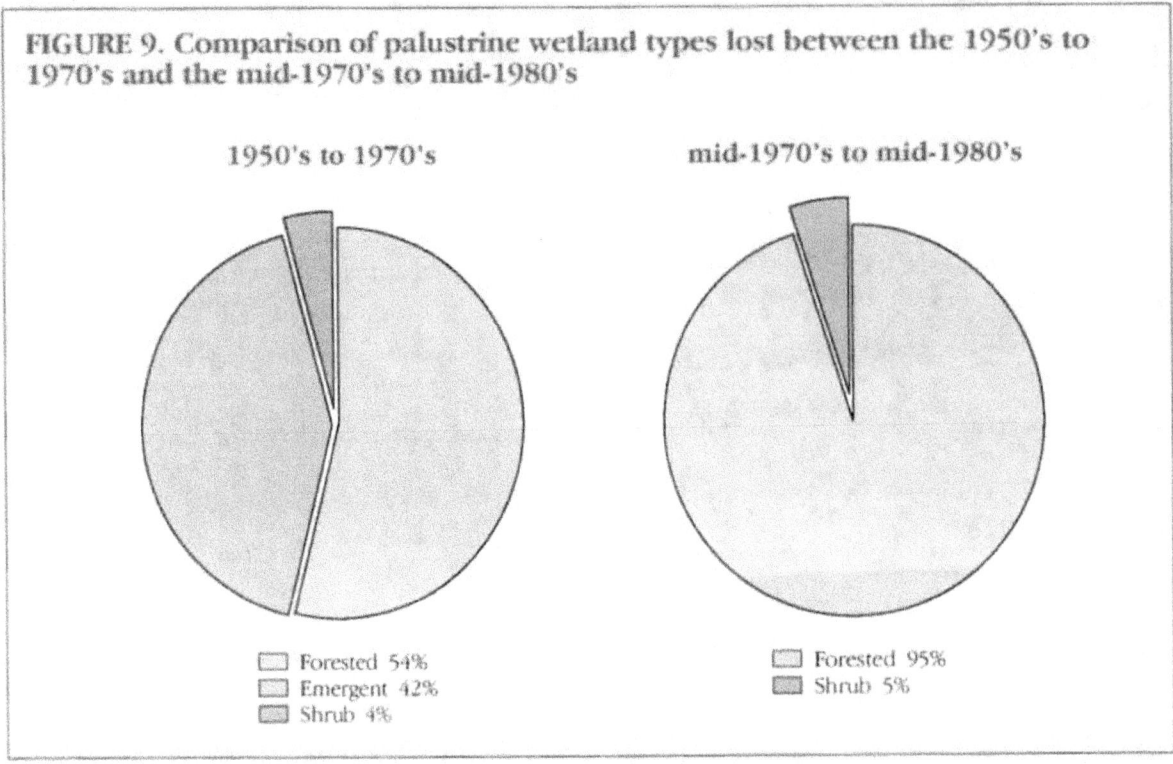

FIGURE 9. Comparison of palustrine wetland types lost between the 1950's to 1970's and the mid-1970's to mid-1980's

1950's to 1970's

mid-1970's to mid-1980's

- ☐ Forested 54%
- ☐ Emergent 42%
- ☐ Shrub 4%

- ☐ Forested 95%
- ☐ Shrub 5%

tional 49.1 thousand acres of palustrine emergent wetlands were converted to non-vegetated wetlands. At the same time, 722.2 thousand acres of palustrine forested wetlands and 68.6 thousand acres of palustrine shrub wetlands were converted to palustrine emergent wetlands. These conversions more than offset the losses in palustrine emergent wetland acreage, from the mid-1970's to the mid-1980's.

Some of the changes in palustrine emergent wetlands during the study period had a regional pattern. The conversions from forested wetlands occurred primarily in the southeastern States, while losses of palustrine emergent marshes to agriculture occurred in the prairie States, California, Florida and Texas. This not only contributed to losses of palustrine forested wetlands, but also helped mask some of the conversions of palustrine emergent wetlands to upland land use categories.

From the mid-1970's to the mid-1980's, about 249.0 thousand acres of palustrine shrub wetlands were converted to agricultural land uses and 265.0 thousand acres were converted to "other" land uses. These losses were largely offset by the conversion of 482.8 thousand acres of palustrine

forested wetlands to palustrine shrub wetlands (Figure 10). During the study period, there was a net loss of 161.1 thousand acres of shrub wetlands.

From the mid-1970's to the mid-1980's palustrine nonvegetated wetlands increased by 794.0 thousand acres. There were 6.1 million acres of palustrine nonvegetated wetlands in the mid-1980's. Gains in this wetlands category, which were well distributed throughout the conterminous United States, totalled 792.4 thousand acres. Almost all of this increase occurred in palustrine unconsolidated bottoms (primarily ponds) and primarily resulted from ponds built on former upland areas.

Palustrine wetlands acreage in the mid-1970's and mid-1980's was estimated at 100.3 million acres and 97.8 million acres, respectively, with a loss of 2.5 million acres for the study period. The importance of the "other" land use category increased dramatically during this period. Between the mid-1950's to the mid-1970's nearly all (87.0 percent) wetland conversions to upland land uses were due to agriculture. "Other" land use was responsible for about 8.0 percent of the upland conversions. Between the mid-1970's to mid-1980's, upland conversions were more evenly split be-

FIGURE 10. A more complete picture of wetland conversions measured in this study. (All Numbers Are in Thousands)

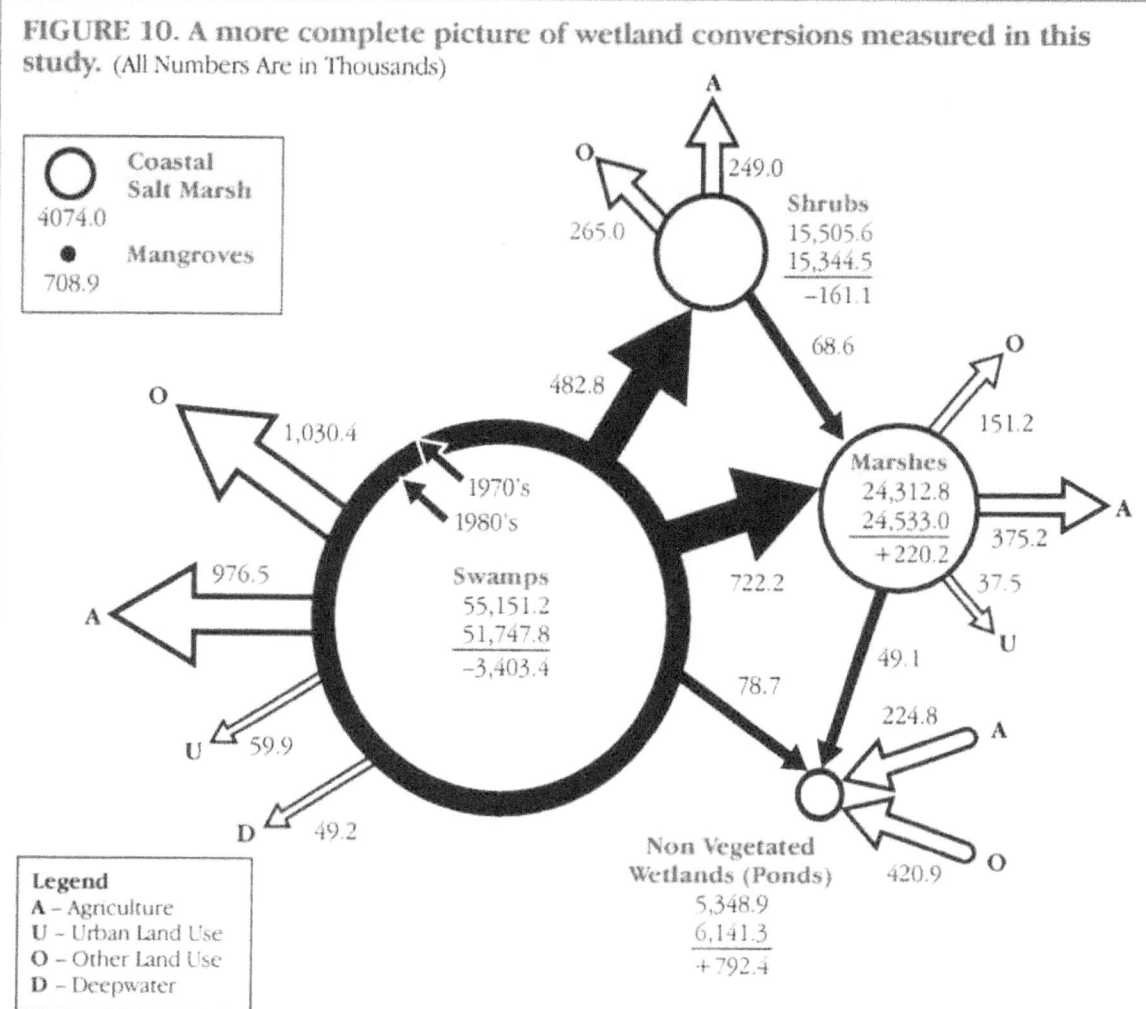

Legend
A – Agriculture
U – Urban Land Use
O – Other Land Use
D – Deepwater

By themselves, estimates of the loss of wetlands between the mid-1970's and the mid-1980's provide an incomplete picture of wetland conversions and losses due to human activity. A more complete picture cannot be appreciated without first understanding that human activities converted millions of acres of wetlands from one category to another during the study period. Through these conversions, some wetland categories increased in acreage at the expense of other wetland categories.

Swamps suffered the greatest loss during the nine-year study period: 3.4 million acres of swamps were lost or converted to other land uses. Over 2.0 million acres of swamps were converted to non-wetlands; most of this acreage was converted to agricultural and "other" land uses.

Large amounts of swamps were also converted to other categories of wetlands: 722.2 thousand acres were converted to marshes, 482.8 thousand acres were converted to shrubs, and 78.7 thousand acres were converted to non-vegetated wetlands.

Although shrubs lost 265.0 thousand acres to the "other" land use category and 249.0 thousand acres to the

agricultural land use category, these losses were nearly offset by the conversion of 482.8 thousand acres of swamps to shrubs. However, despite these gains there was an overall loss of 161.1 thousand acres of shrubs during the study period.

The net gain of 220.2 thousand acres of marshes is similarly deceptive. The 375.2 thousand acres that were lost to agricultural land uses, 151.2 thousand acres that were lost to "other" land uses, and the 37.5 thousand acres lost to urban land uses were more than offset by the conversion of 722.2 thousand acres of swamps and 68.6 thousand acres of shrubs to marshes.

The acreage of non-vegetated wetlands (primarily ponds) increased from 5.3 to 6.1 million acres between the mid-1970's and the mid-1980's. The majority of these gains (420.9 thousand acres) resulted from building ponds on uplands that had not been used for agricultural production, but an additional 224.8 thousand acres were built on former agricultural lands. This category also experienced gains from converted swamps and marsh wetlands.

tween agricultural land use (54.0 percent) and "other" land use (41.0 percent). A substantial portion of lands included in the "other" category were lands that had been drained and cleared of vegetation, but the land had not been put to an identifiable use.

Urban land uses were responsible for an estimated 59.9 thousand acre net loss in palustrine forested wetlands, 37.5 thousand acres of palustrine emergent wetlands, and 21.0 thousand acres of palustrine shrub wetlands, from the mid-1970's to the mid-1980's.

Deepwater Habitats

The changes observed in lacustrine and riverine deepwater habitat acreage between the mid-1970's and the mid-1980's were relatively small (about 0.4 percent). Most of the gains resulted from increases in the lacustrine system and primarily occurred in the southeastern States of Alabama, Florida, Georgia, Mississippi and South Carolina. Although these figures are an indicator of small gains in deepwater habitats, the reliability of the estimate is not sufficient to support definitive comparisons.

SUMMARY

The results of this study document a continuing loss of wetland acreage from the mid-1970's to the mid-1980's. An estimated 1.1 percent of estuarine wetlands and 2.5 percent of inland wetlands were lost from the lower 48 States during the nine-year study period.

An estimated 3.4 million acres of palustrine forested wetlands were lost between the mid-1970's and the mid-1980's. Although gains in other palustrine categories appear to offset some of the overall losses, many of the gains are simply conversions between wetland types. The subsequent report, which is currently in preparation, will more fully analyze and discuss the relationships between wetland losses and gains and shifts between wetland cover type categories.

Agricultural land uses accounted for 54.0 percent of the conversions from wetland to upland. "Other" land uses were responsible for 41.0 percent of these losses. A significant portion of the lands classified as "other" were lands that had been drained and cleared of vegetation, but the land had not been put to an identifiable use. Urban expansion made up the balance of the conversions.

Trends in the estuarine system indicate that estuarine wetlands declined by 1.1 percent over the study period. Most of these losses occurred to estuarine emergent salt marshes along the Gulf Coast States. Estuarine subtidal deepwater increased substantially at the expense of these coastal salt marsh systems.

REFERENCES CITED

Anderson, J.R., E.E. Hardy, J.T. Roach, and R.E. Witmer. 1976. *A land use and land cover classification system for use with remote sensor data.* U.S. Geological Survey Professional Paper 964. U.S. Geological Survey, Washington, D.C. 28 pp.

Barnard, W.D., C.K. Ansell, J. Harn and D. Kevin. 1985. *The use and regulation of wetlands in the U.S.* In: Wetland Protection: Strengthening the role of the States, J.A. Kusler (ed). Assoc. of State Wetland Managers. pp. 27-39.

Cowardin, L.M., V. Carter, F.C. Golet, and E.T. LaRoe. 1979. *Classification of wetlands and deepwater habitats of the United States.* U.S. Fish and Wildlife Service, Washington, D.C. 131 pp.

Dahl, T.E. 1990. *Wetlands losses in the United States 1780's to 1980's.* U.S. Department of the Interior, Fish and Wildlife Service, Washington, D.C. 21 pp.

Dahl, T.E. and H.R. Pywell. 1989. *National status and trends study: Estimating wetland resources in the 1980's.* In: Wetlands: Concerns and Successes. American Water Resources Association Symposium. Tampa, FL. pp. 25-31.

Frayer, W.E., T.J. Monahan, D.C. Bowden, and F.A. Graybill. 1983a. *Status and trends of wetlands and deepwater habitats in the conterminous United States, 1950's to 1970's.* Colorado State University, Fort Collins, CO. 31 pp.

Frayer, W.E., T.J. Monahan, D.C. Bowden, and F.A. Graybill. 1983b. *Procedures for using existing statistical wetland data to determine sample sites needed to produce wetland acreage estimates for selected geographic areas.* Colorado State University, Fort Collins, CO. 8 pp. + Appendix.

Frayer, W.E., D.D. Peters and H.R. Pywell. 1989. *Wetlands of the California Central Valley: Status and trends 1939 to mid-1980's.* U.S. Fish and Wildlife Service, Portland, OR. 27 pp.

Hall, J.V. 1988. *Alaska coastal wetlands survey.* U.S. Fish and Wildlife Service and National Oceanic and Atmospheric Administration Cooperative Report, Washington, D.C. 36 pp.

Hammond, E.H. 1970. *Physical subdivisions of the United States of America.* In: National atlas of the United States of America. U.S. Geological Survey, Washington, D.C. Page 61.

Kusler, J.A. and G. Brooks (eds.) 1987. *Proceedings of the national wetland symposium: Wetland Hydrology.* Association of State Wetland Managers. Berne, NY. 339 pp.

Langbein, W.B. and K.T. Iseri. 1960. *General introduction and hydrologic definitions manual of hydrology. Part 1. General surface water techniques.* U.S. Geological Survey, Water Supply Paper 1541-A. 29 pp.

Mitsch, W.J. and J.G. Gosselink. 1986. *Wetlands.* Van Nostrand Reinhold Co., NY. 539 pp.

Reed, P.B. 1988. *National list of plant species that occur in wetlands: 1988 National Summary.* Biol. Rept. 88 (24). U.S. Fish and Wildlife Service, Washington, D.C. 244 pp.

Shaw, S.P. and C.G. Fredine. 1956. *Wetlands of the United States.* U.S. Department of the Interior, Fish and Wildlife Service, Circular 39. Washington, D.C. 67 pp.

The Conservation Foundation. 1988. *Protecting America's Wetlands: An action agenda.* The final report of the National Wetlands Policy Forum. Washington, D.C. 69 pp.

Tiner, R.W. Jr. 1984. *Wetlands of the United States: current status and recent trends.* U.S. Department of the Interior, Fish and Wildlife Service. Washington, D.C. 59 pp.

Tiner, R.W. Jr. 1987. *Mid-Atlantic Wetlands—A disappearing natural treasure.* U.S. Fish and Wildlife Service and U.S. Environmental Protection Agency cooperative publication. Newton Corner, MA. 28 pp.

U.S.D.A. Soil Conservation Service. 1987. *Hydric Soils of the United States.* U.S. Department of Agriculture, Washington, D.C.

U.S.D.A. Soil Conservation Service, Soil Survey Staff. 1975. *Soil taxonomy: A basic system of soil classification for making and interpreting soil surveys.* Agricultural Handbook 436, U.S. Department of Agriculture, Washington, D.C. 754 pp.

U.S. Fish and Wildlife Service. 1990a. *Wetlands action plan.* Washington, D.C. 31 pp + Appendices.

U.S. Fish and Wildlife Service. 1990b. *Cartographic conventions for the National Wetlands Inventory.* St. Petersburg, FL. 73 pp.

U.S. Fish and Wildlife Service. 1990c. *Photo interpretation conventions for the National Wetlands Inventory.* St. Petersburg, FL. 45 pp. + Appendices.

U.S. Fish and Wildlife Service. 1991. United States Department of the Interior Budget Justifications, F.Y. 1992. Washington, D.C. p.121.

APPENDIX A
GLOSSARY OF CLASSIFICATION TERMINOLOGY
(ADAPTED FROM COWARDIN ET AL. 1979)

Wetland

In general terms, wetlands are lands where saturation with water is the dominate factor determining the nature of soil development and the types of plant and animal communities living in the soil and in its surface. The single feature that most wetlands share is soil or substrate that is at least periodically saturated with or covered by water. The water creates severe physiological problems for all plants and animals except those that are adapted for life in water or in saturated soil.

Wetlands are lands transitional between terrestrial and aquatic systems where the water table is usually at or near the surface or the land is covered by shallow water. For purposes of this classification wetlands must have one or more of the following three attributes: (1) at least periodically, the land supports predominantly hydrophytes,* (2) the substrate is predominantly undrained hydric soil,** and (3) the substrate is nonsoil and is saturated with water or covered by shallow water at some time during the growing season of each year.

The term wetland includes a variety of areas that fall into one of five categories: (1) areas with hydrophytes and hydric soils, such as those commonly known as marshes, swamps, and bogs; (2) areas without hydrophytes but with hydric soils—for example, flats where drastic fluctuation in water level, wave action, turbidity, or high concentration of salts may prevent the growth of hydrophytes; (3) areas with hydrophytes but nonhydric soils, such as margins of impoundments or excavations where hydrophytes have become established but hydric soils have not yet developed; (4) areas without soils but with hydrophytes such as the seaweed-covered portions of rocky shores; and (5) wetlands without soil and without hydrophytes, such as gravel beaches or rocky shores without vegetation.

Drained hydric soils that are now incapable of supporting hydrophytes because of a change in water regime are not considered wetlands by our definition. These drained hydric soils furnish a valuable record of historic wetlands, as well as an indication of areas that may be suitable for restoration.

Marine System

The Marine System consists of the open ocean overlying the continental shelf and its associated high-energy coastline. Marine habitats are exposed to the waves and currents of the open ocean and the water regimes are determined primarily by the ebb and flow of oceanic tides. Salinities exceed 30 parts per thousand, with little or no dilution except outside the mouths of estuaries. Shallow coastal indentations or bays without appreciable freshwater inflow, and coasts with exposed rocky islands that provide the mainland with little or no shelter from wind and waves, are also considered part of the Marine System because they generally support typical marine biota.

Estuarine System

The Estuarine System consists of deepwater tidal habitats and adjacent tidal wetlands that are usually semienclosed by land but have open, partly obstructed, or sporadic access to the open ocean, and in which ocean water is at least occasionally diluted by freshwater runoff from the land. The salinity may be periodically increased above that of the open ocean by evaporation. Along some low-en-

---

* *The U.S. Fish and Wildlife Service has published the list of plants that occur in wetlands of the United States (Reed 1988).*

** *U.S.D.A., Soil Conservation Service has developed the list of hydric soils for the United States (U.S.D.A., Soil Conservation Service, 1987).*

ergy coastlines there is appreciable dilution of sea water. Offshore areas with typical estuarine plants and animals, such as red mangroves (Rhizophora mangle) and eastern oysters (Crassostrea virginica), are also included in the Estuarine System.

Marine and Estuarine Subsystems

Subtidal: The substrate is continuously submerged by marine or estuarine waters.

Intertidal: The substrate is exposed and flooded by tides. Intertidal includes the splash zone of coastal waters.

Palustrine System

The Palustrine System includes all nontidal wetlands dominated by trees, shrubs, persistent emergents, emergent mosses or lichens, and all such wetlands that occur in tidal areas where salinity due to ocean derived salts is below 0.5 parts per thousand. It also includes wetlands lacking such vegetation, but with all of the following four characteristics: (1) area less than 8 ha (20 acres); (2) active wave formed or bedrock shoreline features lacking; (3) water depth in the deepest part of basin less than 2 meters at low water; and (4) salinity due to ocean derived salts less than 0.5 parts per thousand.

Classes

Unconsolidated Bottom: Unconsolidated Bottom includes all wetlands with at least 25 percent cover of particles smaller than stones, and a vegetative cover less than 30 percent. Examples of unconsolidated substrates are: sand, mud, organic material, cobble-gravel.

Aquatic Bed: Aquatic Beds are dominated by plants that grow principally on or below the surface of the water for most of the growing season in most years. Examples include: seagrass beds,* pondweeds (*Potamogeton* spp.) wild celery (*Vallisneria americana*) waterweed (*Elodea* spp.), and duckweed (*Lemna* spp.)

Rocky Shore: Rocky Shore includes wetland environments characterized by bedrock, stones, or boulders which singly or in combination have an areal cover of 75 percent or more and an areal vegetative coverage of less than 30 percent.

Unconsolidated Shore: Unconsolidated Shore includes all wetland habitats having two characteristics: (1) unconsolidated substrates with less than 75 percent areal cover of stones, boulders or bedrock and; (2) less than 30 percent areal cover of vegetation other than pioneering plants.

Emergent Wetland

Emergent Wetlands are characterized by erect, rooted, herbaceous hydrophytes, excluding mosses and lichens. This vegetation is present for most of the growing season in most years. These wetlands are usually dominated by perennial plants.

Shrub Wetland

Shrub Wetlands include areas dominated by woody vegetation less than 6 meters (20 feet) tall. The species include true shrubs, young trees, and trees or shrubs that are small or stunted because of environmental conditions.

Forested Wetland

Forested Wetlands are characterized by woody vegetation that is 6 meters tall or taller.

Deepwater Habitats

Deepwater Habitats are permanently flooded land lying below the deepwater of wetlands. Deepwater habitats include environments where surface water is permanent and often deep, so that water, rather than air, is the principal medium within which the dominant organisms live, whether or not they are attached to the substrate. As in wetlands, the dominant plants are hydrophytes; however, the substrates are considered nonsoil because the water is too deep to support emergent vegetation (U.S.D.A. Soil Conversation Service, Soil Survey Staff 1975).

Riverine System

The Riverine System includes deepwater habitats contained within a channel, with the exceptions habitats with water containing ocean derived salts in excess of 0.5 parts per thousand. A channel is "an open conduit either naturally or artificially

---

* *Although some seagrass beds may be evident on aerial photography, water and climatic conditions often prevent their detection. The data presented in this report should not be interpreted as a reliable indicator of the extent of seagrass acreage in coastal waters.*

created which periodically or continuously contains moving water, or which forms a connecting link between two bodies of standing water" (Langbein and Iseri 1960).

Lacustrine System

The Lacustrine System includes deepwater habitats with all of the following characteristics: (1) situated in a topographic depression or a dammed river channel; (2) lacking trees, shrubs, persistent emergents, emergent mosses or lichens with greater than 30 percent coverage; (3) total area exceeds 8 ha (20 acres). Similar wetland and deepwater habitats totaling less than 8 ha are also included in the Lacustrine System if an active, wave-formed or bedrock shoreline feature makes up all or part of the boundary, or if the water depth in the deepest part of the basin exceeds 2 m (6.6 feet) at low water.

Agriculture*

Agricultural Land may be defined broadly as land used primarily for production of food and fiber. Agricultural activity is evidenced by distinctive geometric field and road patterns on the landscape and the traces produced by livestock or mechanized equipment. Examples of agricultural land use include: cropland and pasture; orchards, groves, vineyards, nurseries, and ornamental horticultural areas; confined feeding operations; and other agricultural land.

Urban

Urban or Built-up Land is comprised of areas of intensive use with much of the land covered by structures. Included in this category are cities, towns, villages, strip developments along highways, transportation, power, and communications facilities, and areas such as those occupied by mills, shopping centers, industrial and commercial complexes.

Other Land Use

Other Land Use is composed of uplands not fitting into the first two upland categories. It includes Anderson's Level I classes of forest land, range

land, and barren land. Typically these lands would include range land or native prairie; upland forests and scrub lands; strip mines and quarries; and barren land.

In addition to the preceding definitions, several of the individual wetland categories were grouped in this document for discussion purposes. These terms, which appear in some of the tables and figures in this document, are defined as follows:

Wetlands and deepwater habitats include all marine, estuarine, palustrine, riverine, and lacustrine classifications.

Wetlands include estuarine, marine and palustrine wetlands.

Deepwater habitats include estuarine subtidal, riverine, and lacustrine habitats.

Estuarine wetlands include all estuarine intertidal categories.

Estuarine nonvegetated wetlands include estuarine intertidal unconsolidated shore and aquatic beds.

Estuarine vegetated wetlands include estuarine intertidal emergent, forested, and scrub/shrub habitats.

Palustrine wetlands include all palustrine categories.

Palustrine nonvegetated wetlands include unconsolidated bottom, shores, aquatic beds.

Palustrine vegetated wetlands include palustrine emergent, forested, and scrub/shrub wetlands.

---

* *Adapted from Anderson, et al. 1976.*

APPENDIX B

Appendix B presents acreage, in thousands of acres, and the estimated number of acres that changed their wetland classification between the mid-1970's and the mid-1980's. Column 1 (far left side) identifies the mid-1970's classification while the remaining columns identify the mid-1980's classification. Acreage totals for the mid-1970's are in Column 18 (the last column) while acreage totals for the mid-1980's are in the row labeled Total Surfacce Area, mid-1980's (it is the second to the last row). The numbers found in parentheses below the acreage estimates are the standard errors of the estimated acreage expressed as a percentage; asterisks indicate a percent standard error greater than 95 percent.

In the example below, 100,396.0 acres that had been classified as Marine intertidal wetlands in the mid-1970's had the same classification in the mid-1980's. An estimated 583.0 acres that had been classified as Estuarine subtidal wetlands in the mid-1970's were classified as Marine intertidal wetlands in the mid-1980's. An estimated 1,594.0 acres that had been classified as Estuarine intertidal emergent wetlands in the mid-1970's were classified as Marine intertidal wetlands in the mid-1980's. The percent standard errors for these estimates were, respectively, 22.8, 68.1, and 39.9.

Mid-1970's Classification	*Marine* *Intertidal*
Marine Intertidal	100,396.0 (22.8)
Estuarine Subtidal	583.0 (68.1)
Estuarine Intertidal Emergent	1,594.0 (39.9)

Appendix B.

Mid-1970's Classification	Marine		Estuarine				Riverine	Lacustrine
	Intertidal	Subtidal	Intertidal Emergent	Forested/Shrub	Unconsolidated Shore/Rocky Shore	Aquatic Bed		
Marine Intertidal	100,396.0 (22.8)	374.0 (88.2)	1,413.0 (89.1)	15.0 (93.3)	12.0 (*)	0	0	0
Estuarine Subtidal	583.0 (68.1)	18,816,034.0 (2.5)	12,786.0 (20.5)	310.0 (48.1)	19,878.0 (20.3)	302.0 (90.4)	0	10.0 (*)
Estuarine Intertidal Emergent	1,894.0 (39.9)	53,169.0 (13.3)	4,051,577.0 (4.3)	7,345.0 (29.7)	5,788.0 (21.7)	0	0	2,776.0 (61.9)
Estuarine Forested/Shrub	20.0 (*)	1,059.0 (40.6)	3,096.0 (63.8)	690,117.0 (13.6)	289.0 (50.9)	0	0	0
Estuarine Unconsolidated Shore/Rocky Shore	87.0 (64.3)	7,386.0 (18.0)	3,594.0 (22.5)	1,636.0 (52.4)	414,625.0 (12.7)	425.0 (70.4)	188.0 (*)	1,123.0 (67.3)
Estuarine Aquatic Bed	0	57.0 (*)	0	41.0 (*)	6,837.0 (92.1)	240,985.0 (22.2)	0	0
Riverine	0	0	0	0	0	0	5,044,505.0 (10.9)	6,433.0 (*)
Lacustrine	0	0	0	0	0	0	61.0 (*)	57,506,560.0 (11.4)
Palustrine Forested	0	0	23.0 (91.3)	0	0	0	17,979.0 (26.2)	49,412.0 (33.2)
Palustrine Shrub	74.0 (*)	0	109.0 (65.1)	0	4.0 (*)	0	15,605.0 (60.2)	27,818.0 (62.3)
Palustrine Emergent	127.0 (*)	25.0 (*)	0	0	0	0	12,149.0 (32.8)	67,471.0 (24.0)
Palustrine Unconsolidated Shore	0	16.0 (*)	0	16.0 (*)	0	0	0	1,140.0 (76.8)
Palustrine Unconsolidated Bottom	0	109.0 (87.1)	0	0	0	0	357.0 (57.2)	1,897.0 (42.5)
Palustrine Aquatic Bed	0	0	0	0	0	0	202.0 (74.8)	582.0 (74.6)
Agriculture	0	46.0 (*)	0	276.0 (*)	19.0 (94.7)	0	77,921.0 (87.3)	76,190.0 (26.2)
Urban	0	1,765.0 (84.2)	0	0	86.0 (83.7)	0	0	298.0 (91.3)
Other	1,432.0 (52.7)	2,139.0 (28.9)	612.0 (41.8)	251.0 (65.7)	460.0 (37.0)	0	22,326.0 (41.4)	101,098.0 (59.1)
Total surface area, mid-1980's	104,314.0 (22.0)	18,882,182.0 (2.5)	4,074,109.0 (4.3)	709,006.0 (13.4)	447,996.0 (11.9)	241,712.0 (22.1)	5,191,192.0 (11.0)	57,842,800.0 (11.3)
Change mid 1970's to mid 1980's	-203.0 (*)	29,825.0 (31.5)	-70,814.0 (18.2)	15.0 (*)	17,741.0 (42.7)	-6,208.0 (*)	68,176.0 (*)	203,159.0 (48.7)

Appendix B. (cont'd)

Mid-1970's Classification	Mid-1980's Classification									
	Palustrine						Agriculture	Urban	Other	Total
	Forested	Shrub	Emergent	Unconsolidated Shore	Unconsolidated Bottom	Aquatic Bed				
Marine Intertidal	0	803.0 (86.1)	123.0 *	0	0	0	0	0	1,380.0 (43.3)	104,517.0 (22.0)
Estuarine Subtidal	0	35.0 *	140.0 (90.7)	98.0 *	34.0 (67.6)	0	8.0 (87.5)	625.0 (36.0)	1,510.0 (41.9)	1,885,236.0 (2.5)
Estuarine Intertidal Emergent	13.0 (92.3)	0	9,625.0 (53.8)	11.0 (90.1)	377.0 (46.2)	0	3,651.0 (86.7)	2,029.0 (31.9)	6,067.0 (19.1)	4,144,924.0 (4.3)
Estuarine Forested/Shrub	344.0 (94.8)	903.0 (57.3)	256.0 (94.5)	0	49.0 (77.6)	0	329.0 (94.8)	2,473.0 (56.9)	1,059.0 (64.4)	708,991.0 (13.5)
Estuarine Unconsolidated Shore/Rocky Shore	0	0	0	0	0	0	0	90.0 (81.1)	1,101.0 (52.1)	430,255.0 (12.3)
Estuarine Aquatic Bed	0	0	0	0	0	0	0	0	0	247,920.0 (21.8)
Riverine	13,989.0 (34.1)	16,862.0 (29.2)	15,405.0 (38.3)	0	662.0 (65.5)	10 *	1,287.0 (62.1)	0	23,864.0 (61.0)	5,123,015.0 (10.9)
Lacustrine	193.0 (63.2)	4,796.0 (58.2)	96,614.0 (57.4)	180.0 *	773.0 (55.9)	298.0 *	22,693.0 (77.0)	148.0 (70.3)	7,372.0 (57.5)	57,639,652.0 (11.4)
Palustrine Forested	51,128,928.0 (3.4)	1,062,930.0 (10.4)	736,926.0 (12.2)	414.0 (57.5)	64,926.0 (14.4)	13,917.0 (39.1)	979,116.0 (12.0)	59,950.0 (23.3)	1,036,672.0 (17.3)	55,151,184.0 (3.3)
Palustrine Shrub	580,131.0 (22.5)	13,986,549.0 (7.0)	306,555.0 (14.3)	369.0 (60.2)	20,383.0 (16.9)	1,678.0 (27.4)	272,224.0 (27.9)	21,064.0 (37.0)	273,059.0 (40.3)	15,505,618.0 (6.6)
Palustrine Emergent	14,685 (19.7)	238,037.0 (22.0)	22,884,890.0 (8.1)	1,157.0 (65.6)	58,233.0 (12.3)	4,349.0 (31.6)	819,436.0 (13.8)	37,706.0 (40.2)	174,489.0 (41.0)	24,312,752.0 (7.7)
Palustrine Unconsolidated Shore	100.0 (90.0)	731.0 (72.4)	551.0 (66.2)	362,422.0 (36.1)	2,015.0 (42.3)	116.0 (74.1)	217.0 (80.6)	52.0 (84.6)	1,545.0 (36.5)	368,922.0 (35.5)
Palustrine Unconsolidated Bottom	315.0 (38.1)	1,747.0 (29.8)	12,331.0 (16.0)	844.0 (48.7)	4,703,811.0 (23.5)	1,612.0 (28.8)	38,130.0 (22.5)	2,501.0 (42.1)	17,287.0 (24.6)	4,781,379.0 (23.1)
Palustrine Aquatic Bed	52.0 *	45.0 (68.9)	1,713.0 (81.5)	0	1,661.0 (36.7)	194,075.0 (15.1)	23.0 *	15.0 (93.3)	189.0 (74.1)	198,566.0 (14.8)
Agriculture	2,550.0 (55.7)	23,154.0 (39.2)	444,158.0 (82.0)	11,021.0 (68.9)	250,534.0 (17.3)	1,695.0 (39.8)	1,794,428,500			1,795,928,200
Urban	123.0 *	138.0 *	247.0 (38.1)	213.0 (77.0)	2,892.0 (32.4)	29.0 (79.3)				
Other	6,277.0 (45.0)	8,146.0 (61.8)	23,302.0 (27.4)	10,452.0 (25.0)	428,771.0 (41.2)	1,120.0 (57.3)				
Total Surface Area, mid-1980's	51,747,692.0 (3.4)	15,344,877.0 (6.4)	24,532,836.0 (8.6)	387,180.0 (34.0)	5,535,079.0 (20.4)	218,901.0 (13.8)	1,798,238,500			1,983,498,368.0
Change in Acreage mid-1970's to mid-1980's	-3,403,492.0 (8.9)	-160,745.0 *	220,081.0 *	18,258.0 (46.5)	753,699.0 (36.7)	20,345.0 (29.8)	2,310,300			0

CORRECTION TO THE MID-1970'S WETLAND ACREAGE

In 1982, analysis of the first status and trends data indicated that there were 99.0 million acres of wetlands remaining in the conterminous United States as of the mid-1970's. These results were reported by Frayer et al. (1983) and by Tiner (1984). This estimate, which was based on the results of photo interpretation of mid-1970's aerial photography, was inaccurate because of limitations in the imagery that was used.

At the time of that initial study, an effort was made to identify wetland habitats using the best aerial photography available. Much of the imagery available for the earlier status and trends study was black and white photography, which often does not adequately show some categories of forested wetlands (see aerial photographs). Since forested wetlands make-up a large percentage of the national total (50 percent in the mid-1970's), the earlier study underestimated the amount of wetlands remaining in the mid-1970's.

This problem has been corrected in this updated report by using superior quality (i.e., superior quality and color infrared) 1980's imagery to determine an accurate wetland acreage total for the mid-1970's. In the cases where wetlands were identified on the mid-1980's photographs but not on the mid-1970's photographs and where there was no obvious land use change, the mid-1970's wetland acreage was adjusted to reflect the omission. As a result of this re-analysis, the new wetlands estimate for the mid-1970's is 105.9 million acres of wetlands. This correction factor does not invalidate the estimated losses for the mid-1950's to mid-1970's. In fact, it is likely that the losses were even greater than previously estimated because of wetlands that may have been undetected.

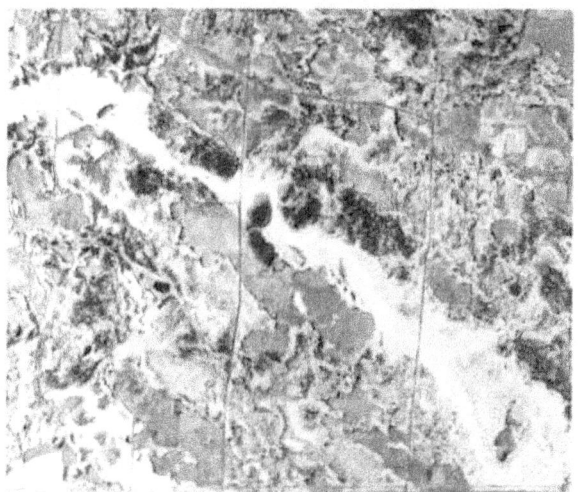

1976

1981